*Suggestions for the consideration of lecturers
and others concerned with teaching in higher education*

D1435536

ESSAYS

Barbara Cockburn
Alec Ross

Teaching in Higher Education Series
ISSN 0309-3565

No.8: Essays
ISBN 0-90169960-8
© School of Education, University of Lancaster

Published by School of Education, University of Lancaster,
Bailrigg, Lancaster, LA1 4YL, England.

Printed in England by Titus Wilson, Kendal.

FOREWORD

This booklet is one of a series produced with the aid of
a grant from the University Grants Committee as part of
its programme for the development of knowledge about and
skill in teaching in higher education. The series is
intended to bring together traditional wisdom (not a
source to be neglected) research findings when available
and relevant, and summaries of what is regarded by the
informed as good practice.

The sub-title "Suggestions for the consideration of
those concerned ..." echoes that of a famous manual for
the guidance of elementary school teachers and this
series shares the same purpose. The handbooks may at
times be mildly hortatory but they are not meant to be
prescriptive. Teaching is something of an art and the
aim is to encourage, within sensible limits, something
of a personal style. The "rules" (if such they be)
are constantly broken by successful teachers but few,
if any, get away with breaking all the rules all the
time.

Universities and other institutions of higher education
have traditionally accepted research and teaching as
their principal functions. The systems developed for
training in research are well worked out. Till now
little has been done for teaching. The initiative
taken by the University Grants Committee was widely
welcomed and has led to an increasing awareness in
higher education generally of the importance of giving
to the teaching function the attention it deserves.
This series is intended to offer help to those who wish
to make an effort to improve their teaching. It is
hoped that those who read these pages will, as a result,
be better prepared for this important aspect of their
daily work.

The authors would be glad to receive reports and
illustrative material which readers may wish to send
with a view to improving the next edition of these
booklets.

C.F. CARTER
Vice-Chancellor
University of Lancaster.

CONTENTS

INTRODUCTION

As he works on students' essays a university or college tutor is, surely, close to the heart of the ill-defined teaching and learning process. Every student who is responsive to the subject he is studying or to its teaching is intimately engaged with it as he writes an essay; nowhere is the relationship between teacher, taught and subject closer. Too often when essays are discussed in the literature of higher education it is in terms of their relative effectiveness as an examining technique; too rarely is space given to discussion of the traditional place of the essay - the means whereby, whether it be part of the terminal assessment or not, the student is given the opportunity of getting close to his subject, of demonstrating what he has learned and showing how he can apply what he knows to new situations. There is a tendency to underplay the traditional use of the essay as a means of learning and of teaching. If we can explain an idea or process clearly we are more confident in our understanding of it; if we teach a student who can explain things well we are encouraged to think that our efforts are not without success.

An essay has been described[1] as a "relatively free and extended response to a problematic situation" and many teachers, with what it would not be inappropriate to call loving care, mull over the problems students might explore in their essays. Whether titles are chosen by himself or negotiated with his students, the search for good essay questions is a particularly enjoyable task for the keen lecturer; not for him the quick riffle

through a pack of used titles of proven serviceability.
He sets out, too, to mark every essay with equal
thoroughness, knowing that, whatever its quality, each
essay is of real importance to its author; not for him
the practised skimming through all but the occasional
essay of distinction.

But, the experienced practitioner will remark, there
are so many essays to set and to mark each term and
then there are the examination questions to work out as
well; how are enough topics of equal interest and
equivalent difficulty to be found? Should one avoid
the overlap between term essays and the questions set in
examinations? Is the answer different when essays
'count' as coursework? Should everyone tackle the
same questions? So many different kinds of essay could
be written on the same theme; how is justice to be done
to them all? Even the lecturer who is least well-
informed about research on assessment knows that both
his attention and the quality of his judgment waver
during long hours spent working through a tide of undergraduate essays. What kind of pragmatic compromise
should he make between the ideal practices he might wish
to adopt and what he is actually willing and able to do?

We begin in Part I: "The Use of Essays" with an examination of what an essay is and how best to use it. Essays
have two clear but not always separate functions: a
teaching-learning function and an assessment function.
This assessment may be formal, as is the case when essays
are given a mark which contributes to the final classification, or informal, when although the essay may not
formally 'count' it is part of the process whereby the

tutor arrives at an estimate of the student's academic quality. We discuss these together with the different types of essay in common use, and the kinds of ability and topic that can be assessed in essays. Questions must be set and titles chosen with properly thought out purposes clearly in mind.

In Part II: "Setting Questions" we look at the choice and timing of coursework essays. We discuss in detail the phrasing and formulation of questions and titles before going on to practical criteria for use in determining how good a question is. This part concludes with a checklist for reviewing essay questions.

Part III: "Marking" sets out the kind of simple systematic procedure for marking essays which can be used by the tutor too inexperienced to be able to mark each essay as he comes to it entirely by impression. We then raise questions which we think every new examiner should consider before he marks a single essay - they are to do with the standards applied to undergraduate essays. Essays are difficult to mark consistently; we look at the practical implications of their unreliability as an examining technique. Lastly we discuss not just marking but commenting on students' essays in preparation for returning them. Habit often becomes master here and too little thought may be given to the influence and the impact a tutor's remarks may have on individual students and their learning.

Does the lecturer's responsibility end with marking? Some students fail to do justice to themselves through lack of the skills essay writing requires. In Part IV:

"Essay Writing" we briefly describe some of the ways in which teachers in higher education might, and arguably should, give help.

Lastly, in the Appendix, we give examples of essay titles and examination questions. We hope this booklet will be read in conjunction both with the Appendix and with examples of your own. Those examples discussed in the text which are not in the Appendix have been made up to suit our purpose or have been supplied by colleagues. Most of the items in the Appendix have been taken from finals papers of the University of Lancaster. We are grateful to the departments concerned for permission to use them.

PART I

THE USE OF ESSAYS

1. WHAT IS AN ESSAY?

What is an essay? The root of the word lies in the
active verbs "to try" or "to attempt" - essentially the
undergraduate essayist 'has a go' for himself at
putting into words what he has been learning. The
academic essay has been formally described by Sims[1]
as "a relatively free and extended written response to
a problematic situation or situations (question or
questions), which intentionally or unintentionally
reveals information regarding the structure, dynamics
and functioning of the student's mental life as it has
been modified by a particular set of learning experiences".
It is a cumbersome definition but accurate, and worth
looking at more closely.

A relatively free response
An essay contrasts with tests (like an objective test)
whose questions are intended to elicit a single correct
response predetermined by the author of the test. But
the response allowed to the essayist is only relatively
free. Often, indeed, it would seem from the way in
which a title or question is framed that the scope and
content of the expected essay has been fairly rigorously
predetermined. Look, for example, at question 2

in the Appendix.   The relative freedom each student has
in answering this kind of question is his freedom to
answer more or less completely and in his own words.

At the opposite pole are questions like 10, 14 and 27 in
the Appendix, where the students are implicitly invited
to formulate judgments or to examine issues from the
viewpoint of their choice.   Given far greater freedom
of response each student is left to determine for himself what the full implications of the question are,
and how he is to tackle it.   Most undergraduate essays,
essay-type examination questions in particular, avoid
the extremes in either direction, being designed to
give scope for the abler students while indicating the
main ground each essay should cover.   The art is to do
this without signposting the way towards stereotyped
answers.   See question 13 in the Appendix, for example.

Most essays written on the same topics or in answer to
the same examination question will be about substantially
the same things.   Nevertheless, in higher education we
are particularly concerned with what is distinctive
about each student's essay: the particular points he
has made, how he has related them, the way in which his
essay is organised, the value he attaches to different
aspects of a subject.   The freedom of response an essay
allows makes this an indispensable teaching medium and
means of assessment.

Sims[1] has further suggested that when an essay is
deliberately given a vague title it can serve as a
"projective test".   The essay reveals the characteristic
ways in which individuals structure situations.   When

forced to make value judgments (some of which a student
has been taught to make, some of which he makes instinct-
ively) the student projects himself into the essay reveal-
ing the style and quality of his mind.

An extended response
An essay is essentially an extended response and titles
and examination questions are designed to encourage
students to answer at length; "Give them enough rope ...".
But restrictions may be placed both on the length of an
essay and on the period of time allowed for writing it.

For example, for teaching purposes students may be
asked to write several essays of varying length and
complexity. These could provide practice in basic
essay writing skills and exercise students' ability at
the one extreme to research a topic thoroughly and
meticulously, and to handle a mass of material, and at
the other extreme to concentrate their thinking and
to economise in expression. The number and length of
assignments set relates to the needs and capacities of
students at different levels of a course. Similarly
in an examination, short answers may specifically be
requested for a number of questions designed to provide
a measure of the students' mastery of factual knowledge
while they are asked to spend the whole of another
examination session answering one question which allows
them to display the full range and depth of their understanding of a subject. (The characteristics of different
forms of essay are listed on pages 6-7, their uses are
discussed in the latter part of this section.)

The time allowed for each essay is obviously a function

of the length of the essay required and of the type of
essay or of examination answer the students are expected
to submit.   Thus only 5-10 minutes may be allowed for
writing the kind of short answer examination question
referred to above, three hours being given for the more
comprehensive question.   Any question which requires
thought must be allowed sufficient time for students of
all abilities adequately to come to grips with the
problem.   A self-evident point which bears constant
repetition is that if an examination using essays is
designed to discriminate between students of different
abilities on the grounds of their knowledge and understanding of a subject then the examination must not give
undue advantage to those who think and who write quickly.
There are those, of course, who feel that quick thinking
is a discriminatory characteristic between the able and
the less able, but that is another argument.

Where non-examination essays are concerned consideration
must be given to all the demands on students' time (such
as formal teaching and other assignments on other courses)
and to the availability of resources which students must
share.   For example access to library books in limited
supply may be restricted.   Adequate time must therefore
be allowed for every student to read as widely and to
research a topic as thoroughly as their tutor expects
them to do.

A written response
Since essays are always a written response and students
are expected, for the most part, to use their own words,
then success in essay writing is always to some degree
dependent on literary ability.   Writing essays can be

a means of acquiring command of language and the art of communicating ideas clearly and persuasively.   A lecturer has a responsibility for initiating the novice into the skills he himself has mastered.   Development of the ability to formulate ideas and to express critical judgments is integral to the study of many subjects.

The extent to which literary style enters into the judgment which tutors, formally or informally, make, will vary according to the subject.   In all subjects, including those with a highly developed technical language, the tutor should look for clarity and accuracy of expression; the scientific report which is not clear and coherent is by definition non-professional.   The essay should always demonstrate the most important element of good design - it should be well adapted to its purpose.

Good ideas deserve clear and elegant expression; yet no amount of elegant expressiveness should be allowed to compensate for ideas which have not been properly thought through.

A response to a problematic situation
The problematic situation, the central point, the question posed in the title of an essay, may be more or less familiar to the students but it should be put in such a way as to exercise their wits.   The task set for the essayist may range from a particular target he is expected to hit to a far-reaching problem, or set of problems, he is expected to analyse and which may be open to resolution in many and often complex ways.   Sometimes the problem is perennial; sometimes solutions are to be found in the literature.   A problem may be real or

imaginary. It may be familiar, having already been discussed in seminars or expounded in lectures and texts, or it may be relatively unfamiliar and, instead of having a go at presenting studied responses in a coherent and logical manner, the student must try to resolve an issue for himself by applying what he has learned. There may be no problem of any substance at all except insofar as writing an essay is in itself a problem; students may be asked to give a relatively straightforward account of a topic. Much depends on what you wish to use an essay for and that to a significant extent depends on the point in the course in which it is used.

Before we go on to discuss the essay's two main functions - in teaching and learning, and in assessment - here is a summary of the common forms an essay can take.

2. TYPES OF ESSAY

i) <u>Coursework essays</u>
Short essays, essay outlines or seminar notes of, perhaps, 500 words.
Standard essays or full seminar papers of anything from 1,000-2,500 words.
Extended essays of 2,500-5,000 words.
Dissertations of anything from 5,000-15,000 words.
(A dissertation is sometimes akin to a very substantial extended essay, sometimes closer to a thesis.)

The subject of an essay tends to increase in complexity, though the central question does not necessarily become at the same time more open-ended, as it increases in length.

ii) <u>Examination essays</u>
Short answer essay papers may require students
to answer perhaps 10-20 questions in 3 hours.
(This estimate is based on the traditional
"gobbet" question: 3-5 "gobbets" to a question,
3-4 questions in 3 hours.)
Traditional papers require students to write
3-4 essay answers in 3 hours.   (Less commonly
the time allowed may be a prescribed number of
days.)
Special papers often require students to write
one essay in 3 hours.

Any examination may consist of unseen, prior notice or
open book questions.   (See "Inside Assessment".)   The
questions tend to become more open-ended, that is, the
candidates are given greater freedom of response, as the
number of questions in a paper decreases.

3. ESSAYS IN TEACHING AND LEARNING

We have to separate coursework essays from examinations
in this section, for examination essays are, of course,
usually only of direct use to teachers.   The evidence
which marked papers provide, when they are available,
analysed at leisure, may be a useful guide to the design
of long term teaching strategies.   But to be of use in
current courses and to be of direct benefit to students
feedback has to be immediate and can therefore only be
supplied by essays written during and not at the end of
course units.

Written sequentially during a course of study essays

provide invaluable evidence both of how much material
the students have covered and of their growth in understanding.   They may also show up the strengths and
weaknesses of teaching events and of courses.   Essays
may therefore show:
* how effective teaching has been;
* the progress in learning made collectively by
a class;
* the extent and depth of each student's learning.

Take the individual student first.   It is not only his
relative success in tackling different topics or problems
which will guide his future studying but the interest
aroused by his engagement with them.   What would he
like to do and what is he able to take on?   The writing
of essays coupled with discussion with a tutor can direct
a student towards:
* further reading (either complementary to a
taught course or for independent study in
parallel with it);
* topics for future essays or dissertations;
* his choice of options within a current course;
* his choice of subsequent courses;
* his post-graduate career.
(For a discussion of the negative effects the use of
essays for assessment may have on students' learning
see Thomas.)[2]

Next we take the tutor or lecturer.   Students' essays
may collectively provide evidence of what has been
satisfactorily learned and be the base on which subsequent teaching events are constructed.   They give
some indication of whether teaching has been pitched at

the right level.   They may also show both teachers and students what has not been achieved - what has been mis-understood and what has not been adequately covered. Here, then, is a guide to the possible need for:

* compensatory reading, additional practical work, revision, or remedial tuition;
* fuller expositions, the need for further discussion or more illustrative examples to clarify difficult points;
* restructuring or even rethinking a course unit: changing the pattern of emphasis on different topics; altering the balance between, say, expository and discussion methods of teaching; increasing the amount of information students are given concerning what the course is about, what kind of work is expected of them, and how much time is allocated to private studying, formal teaching events and writing essays.

The standard 2,000 word essay is still the most satis-factory source of evidence both about what students have learned of what they were expected to have learned and at the same time about unanticipated gaps in their learning.   Less ambitious short written exercises in essay form or related to essays may also be used more frequently to monitor the acquisition of specific skills or bodies of knowledge.   (See page 15.)

4. ESSAYS FOR COURSEWORK ASSESSMENT

Traditionally a clear distinction has been made on the one hand between "the essay", i.e. the weekly or fort-

nightly paper written by the student for - and perhaps
read to - the tutor, which is commented on but often
not formally marked and on the other the "exam question"
i.e. the short essay written under examination conditions
which is never commented on but which is carefully marked,
perhaps double-marked, and is used to place the student
in his class.   Certain criteria are common to each type
but others are not.   For example, precise references
are required in the one but not the other - we look at
criteria of this kind in Part III.

In many universities and colleges this practice continues
unchanged but in others the distinction has been blurred.
There are essays done in term time which are part of the
"continuous" or "coursework" assessment which itself
forms part of the final assessment.   Those nurtured in
the first tradition find difficulty in adapting to the
second.   What was once the vehicle for teaching has now
become the means of assessment and the lecturer is put
in the equivocal position of being both tutor and
examiner at one and the same time.   All teachers in
higher education are accustomed to changing their role
at the end of the course when they become examiners;
many find it difficult to do so during the course.

The use of essays in assessment procedures leads to
further problems, not all of them fully thought through,
particularly where there is heavy reliance on course
essays for assessment.   Since essays are on one topic
only, and since four or five essays in the course of a
year might be all that is required for any one course,
coverage cannot be complete.   (It is not uncommon for,
say, 5 out of 8 essays which have been written to be

selected for formal submission.)[4]   In such situations
some tutor/examiners strive for essay titles which thrust
the student into situations calling for a wide survey or
which are aimed at the elucidation of widely relevant
principles.   (Would you use the more open examples in
the Appendix as the titles for coursework essays or as
examination questions?)

Students may sometimes, too, rework their essays, or
some of their essays, with tutorial guidance before
submission.[2]   This practice illustrates how closely
the role of essays in teaching and in assessment overlap.   It also illustrates one of the difficulties
which may arise when well-tutored essays are offered as
part of the terminal assessment.

5. ESSAY-TYPE EXAMINATIONS

The short essay written as part of a formal examination
is related to but different from the essay - whether
it be formally assessable or not - written in the course
of the year.   This is not the place to discuss the
merits of the "Answer 3 questions in 3 hours" type of
examination paper but the answer written by the student
in traditional papers of this kind is, in fact, an essay,
albeit of a special kind and written under somewhat
artifical conditions.

There is a choice of questions in traditional examinations.   In order to avoid the possibility of some
students being assessed on too restricted a base, if
questions are going to be fairly narrow, or if individual examiners are given complete freedom to ask whatever

kind of question they wish, then it may be necessary to
control choices so that all students are examined over
a comparable range. We all deplore question-spotting
and when examiners give candidates greater freedom of
choice in examinations than they normally have in the
courses of study they follow, then control of the scope
and direction of individual questions may be necessary
in the interests of achieving reasonable coverage of the
syllabus.

Another facet of the problem of the dual use of the
essay - as a mode of teaching and a method of examining -
is the question of whether or not it is fair to use
essay-type examinations in all subjects. If it is
decided to use the essay to achieve particular teaching
objectives then it is right to include essays in the
terminal assessment to test how well these objectives
have been met. If it is decided to use essay-type
examinations in the terminal assessment then fairness
demands that students should be provided with experience
of - indeed training in - essay writing during the course.

6. THE ESSAY AS AN INSTRUMENT OF ASSESSMENT

Essays are imperfect instruments of assessment. This
is mainly because they are difficult to mark consistently.
(The reliability of essays is discussed in Part III).
Reliability is important; it affects the validity, that
is the degree to which a test is effective in measuring
what it is intended to measure. A test which can be
marked with absolute consistency is not necessarily one
with high validity, but high validity is not possible
when reliability is low. Because of the difficulty of

marking essays consistently, then, it becomes that much more important to observe as many of the other conditions for high validity as possible. (These are discussed in some detail in "Inside Assessment".) Double marking, preferably blind, is always to be recommended when the essay forms a significant part of the total assessment.

An examiner must have good grounds for choosing essays as the method of assessment and should further have clear and explicit intentions in mind when setting each question or assignment. If he is clear about the point of each question he is more likely to be able to ensure that the phrasing of the question is unambiguous and does not belie his intentions, and that the marks given for individual essays do relate to what the examiner, or the tutor/examiner, intended should be assessed. Part II of this booklet deals with setting questions, Part III with marking. Here we look more closely at what examiners may intend to assess.

What is to be examined?
In those subjects open to objective testing (see "The Use of Objective Tests") a detailed specification can be drawn up for an examination which, ideally, will closely match the structure and specification of a course syllabus. In areas of study like the humanities where essays are the preferred mode of assessment a teacher may be justly confident that he knows what he intends to assess though he cannot often break this down into particulars of content and attributes, of knowledge and abilities. An essay is a relatively free response; content and qualities cannot be pre-determined in detail even when the examiner seeks to

elicit a specific type of response.

This being said, every new examiner should nevertheless give careful thought to just what it is he is examining by means of essays. It is not enough to say that he expects different patterns of an integration of knowledge, understanding and abilities to which he will give a rating when he is presented with each essay. In framing questions he should be anticipating the general run of responses.

Essays could be used specifically to examine narrow issues or separately to assess different abilities. For example, an essay could be intended to assess the ability to present an argument. The framing of the question will then preclude any general discussion about arguments or of the relative importance of different arguments; students will be explicitly instructed to set out the argument in question in full. Thus "Give the reasons for ...", "Show how the principle X may be deduced from ...", "Explain in detail why ...".

Similarly an essay question designed specifically to assess the ability to integrate information from a wide range of sources does not implicitly invite students to give their own views by beginning simply "Discuss". However, where other methods could be used to assess the achievement of more limited and precise objectives perhaps they should be. The essay is the method of choice where unreliability is accepted because the examiner wishes to make the kind of comprehensive assessment which requires students to make a "relatively free and extended response to a problematic situation".

14

Where the essay format is always used, from habit, then more use might be made of reduced forms of essay. For example, short answer essay tests can be used to assess simple mastery of the content of a course; the examiner's questions can be limited and precise but students are still assessed on their ability to organise and to set out their answers for themselves.

Another example would be the use of essay outlines. It may be as difficult to compare and contrast essay outlines written by different students, say, specifically for the purpose of assessing their ability to organise what they know in response to a given question, as it is comparatively to assess their full essays. One student may offer a well organised but slight essay, another may outline a vast mass of material. Examiners may disagree about what is or is not well organised. [3] But a clearer idea of each student's organising ability might be got from examination of a number of essay outlines and from comparison of these with similar sets of outlines from other students, than is to be had from examination of single essays.

7. ESSAYS FOR ASSESSMENT: THEIR BEST USE

The distinction between essays as a teaching medium and essays as instruments of assessment is becoming blurred; in this section we ignore it. We do not rehearse the arguments for and against the use of coursework for assessment; these arguments are to be heard in common rooms, they may be formally discussed in boards of studies, they are thoroughly examined in the literature. We do assert that, however essays and essay-type examination questions are used, they should be part of a balanced assessment scheme.   Examiners may use different methods for different specific purposes.   What may essays best be used for?

The great strength of the essay as an examining technique lies in the scope it gives to each student for setting out what he knows in his own way and for deciding, with relative freedom, what points are important and relevant to the questions he is asked.   The good traditional searching essay question should be used to make comprehensive estimations of each student's overall grasp of a subject and of his distinctive abilities.   Unhappily there is often a traditional insistence that every essay question fits this mould when the most cursory reading of sets of papers shows that narrow or trivial questions, or questions demanding only simple factual recall, can pass muster.

Essay-type assessment, whether it be coursework or examination, has other notable virtues.   At their best essays exercise the kind of higher order intellectual abilities lecturers wish to foster; the existence of final examinations in essay form means that students are aware of and try to cultivate such abilities. Essays seem to be a particularly effective goal for students' studying. [3]   Studying with assessment by essay in mind students have been shown, in one research study, to be better prepared for all-round assessment by any method than they were when they prepared for fixed response testing. [5]

Here now is a summary of the possible uses of different forms of essay for assessment purposes.

i) <u>Short answer essays</u> examine mastery of facts,
   principles, single concepts.   They may be used
   as exercises in diagnosis or analysis.[6]

ii) <u>Essay outlines</u> examine the ability to
   organise material, to construct coherent
   arguments, to select relevant information
   from a wide field of study.

iii) <u>Standard essays</u> examine the ability to describe
   and to analyse the relationship between ideas
   and events; to give a coherent account of a
   topic; to select and to weigh evidence in
   support of an argument; to diagnose and to
   suggest solutions to problems; to solve
   familiar types of problem; to express
   critical judgments; to make comparisons.

iv) <u>Extended essays</u> allow the examiner to present
   a more complex problematic situation or one
   that requires more extensive preparation or
   research.

v) <u>Extended time essays</u> allow students to think
   deeply about the problematic situation and therefore can be used to examine the ability to solve
   less familiar problems, to analyse or critically
   to appraise less familiar material.

vi) <u>Dissertations</u> examine the ability to make an
   integrated study in depth over a wide field.

vii) <u>Essays that allow complete freedom of response</u>
   examine the ability to reach independent conclusions, to create a new synthesis of ideas and
   events, or to set out and justify new ideas or
   interpretations.

PART II

SETTING QUESTIONS

1. WHO CHOOSES THE TITLE?

There is never usually any doubt about who chooses examination questions (but see[7]). Students often have some say in the choice of coursework essay titles. They can share in this choice in several ways.

* A list of titles can be prepared by the tutor: each student selects one.

* A list of topics is prepared by the tutor: each student negotiates the precise title of the essay he will write on one of these topics.

* A list of questions is prepared by the tutor: each student negotiates how one of these, or related questions or responsive statements, can be modified to become the title of his essay.

* Students are free to propose their own titles.

Note that lists of topics, questions or quotations can often be arranged to show the relationship between topics or the development of a subject and thus to reinforce the structure of a course unit. On the other hand, the juxtaposition of conflicting statements might spark off productive thinking about a subject.

2. TIMING COURSEWORK ESSAYS

The timing of coursework essays - when you introduce
titles, when you mark essays, when you discuss them -
will be intimately related to the way in which you
teach.   For example, if your course is, roughly
speaking, problem-centred, then you may wish your
students to be conscious from the beginning that these
central problems can fruitfully be looked at from a
number of different angles.   Possible titles for essays
will then be brought to their attention early in the
course.   "You are required to write two essays in this
part of Course 302.   The deadline is the first week of
the Lent Term.   As always you can negotiate a particular
title to suit your own interests but make sure that it
does not overlap unduly with the rest of your degree
studies.   I shall make suggestions from time to time,
but here are some, covering the early part of the course,
to be considering". [8]

On the other hand, if you wish essays to be the product
of mature retrospective consideration of a field of study
as a whole, you may prefer students to focus their
attention on particular themes and issues only on com-
pletion of a course unit.

The timing of essays can be a delicate matter.   Ideally
a teacher asks for essays at a point when, in his judgment, students have spent long enough absorbing and
discussing ideas and information.   Learning to suspend
judgment is part of an academic education;   a tutor
would wish his students to write essays when, and only
when, in terms of the progress of a study, they have

together arrived at a point where it is desirable for
the students now to commit themselves to a viewpoint.
It is regrettable that the demands of timetables,
assessment requirements and the need to consider students'
overall workloads mean that in practice essays are
usually set by clockwork.

Of course, sometimes it is advantageous, from a teaching
viewpoint, to synchronise essays with a teaching time-
table and to use them to monitor the step by step
acquisition of understanding.

In the timing of essays there is tension between their
use in teaching and learning and their role in assessment.   The coursework essays which are formally submitted are often terminal essays; given a choice
tutors will often support this, preferring that essays
(usually those best suited to teaching purposes) written
during a course should not be formally assessed.   Yet
when it is only terminal essays that are assessed
students direct their main efforts to them.

3. FORMULATING TITLES AND QUESTIONS

There is no better introduction to the art of setting
questions than reading sets of examination papers -
lists of coursework essay titles too, when you can find
them.   Papers in your own or allied subjects will teach
you most about, for example, the pin-pointing of examin-
able issues or the way in which familiar topics can
furnish.intellectually challenging questions when
presented from an unusual viewpoint.   You may learn
more about phrasing questions, on the other hand, if

you read papers from quite different areas of study;
freed from absorption in the content, you will be able
to view the form of questions with a more critical eye.

It is of the utmost importance, of course, that
examination questions in particular should be as clearly
and as economically expressed as is possible.   But
there is a traditional language of examining which,
carelessly used, may communicate the examiner's intentions
less clearly than he would wish - we discuss the ambi-
guities which may result in relation to what constitutes
a good question on pages 26-28.

Much depends, as has already been said, on the purpose
of the question.   If it is a short question set part-
way through the first year it will have a different
purpose from one set in the finals paper.   It is, of
course, true that a question such as "Give an account
of ..." can be answered at anything from 'O' level
through to a major monograph.   Nevertheless there is
something to be taken note of in the remark that "This
is not an honours question".   Are we looking for the
(merely?) descriptive?   Then "When ..." and "What..."
questions may have their place but we should recognise
the limitations set by the form of such questions.

"How ..." and "Why ..." questions usually aim at a higher
level of cognitive operation; so do "Compare ..." and
"Contrast ..." questions.   "Give an account ..." is non-
specific and those who use this form of question may
defend it by saying "They know what is wanted".   In a
formal examination students should never be in the
position of having to 'suss out' (as they put it) who

wrote the question before being able to answer it.

Both essay titles and examination questions may vary considerably in the extent to which they spell out what is required by way of answers or treatments of the topic. In general the more precise and specific a question is then the longer and more detailed it is; such questions must be phrased with great care for the accuracy with which they will be interpreted. Look at questions 1, 3 and 8 in the Appendix.

Should instructions come at the beginning or at the end of a question? A common form of question is one which presents a passage or quotation either for discussion or to be analysed according to specified criteria. See, for instance, questions 6 and 16 in the Appendix. Where the instructions are elaborate it seems to be customary for them to precede the passage or passages; this order is reversed when you wish the general tone, style and content of the passage to make an impression on the reader's mind before he turns to consideration of just what he is to do with it.

The phrasing of titles and questions is, obviously, a matter of personal and departmental taste and style. "With what justice is X to be regarded as ..." may be more attractive to both you and your students than the simple "Is X ..."; so may "Explore the force of the assertion ..." when compared with "How convincing is ..." But if you have a penchant for more elaborate phrases ask yourself occasionally whether they are always serving the purpose of the question as well as more commonplace ones do.

As a last example we would like to point to the difference between inviting consideration of views and inviting students to express their own judgment. The use of
the pronoun "you" may be misleading. Thus, "What do
you understand by ..." may conventionally mean "What
have you learned is understood by ..." and is not to be
taken literally to mean "What are your own conclusions
about ...". This may seem a trivial point but in large
institutions with large classes it should not be assumed
that every student has the common sense to understand
the distinction, is familiar with the conventional usages
of a discipline, or has assimilated them from three years
of lectures. If you are in doubt, simply include " ...,
in your view,", or "... in your judgment", or rephrase a
question like "What implications do you see in ..." to
read "What are the implications of ...".

Of course, when inviting the consideration of views an
examiner is often actually asking for comparisons between
views. You may sometimes think it better to be more
explicit and, since you will be expecting everyone
to base their answers on X and Y, or the views of X and
Y, then you will name them in the question. Thus,
"Distinguish between the X and Y views/the views of X
and Y ...", or "To what extent do X and Y overlap in
...", "Are X and Y useful descriptions of ...", "Are
the views of X and Y irreconcilable?".

The phrases we have been discussing are all of the
kind an examiner would use when he has decided what kind
of essay he wishes students to write; they are precise,
they may be supported by specification of the field of
reference to be used and the type, even the number, of

examples to be discussed.   However, many of the best
questions cannot be categorised in terms of the kind of
essay expected - this will obviously be true of many of
the more open questions.   Though precise they will
contain no instructions and no specifications.   Far
less care has to be taken over their construction since
form and content are usually inseparable.   Compare, for
instance, question 2 in the Appendix with question 19.

4. THE QUALITY OF A QUESTION

The quality of any question or title cannot properly be
judged without reference to the essays which students
write in response.   However, it is sensible to set all
your questions and titles on one side, perhaps for a day
or two, and then to review them before you present them.

In general, the more precise and specific a question is,
and the shorter the required answer, then the easier it
becomes to assess its effectiveness.   The degree of
difficulty and the discriminatory power of objective
test items can be calculated;   where essays are concerned
only subjective estimates can be made.   This does not
prevent an examiner making a methodical review of his
questions, and we have compiled a checklist he might use
for this purpose similar to that in the companion booklet
on "The Use of Objective Tests".

But first we describe some general characteristics of
good questions.   There is no evidence from research as
to what constitutes a good question and we claim no
authority for our views nor those we quote.   We offer
them because, in common with others,[9] we feel that

24

insufficient attention is paid to the quality of
individual questions.

All good questions should be as _precise_ as the teacher
or examiner intends them to be.   In general we wish
students to get to grips at once with the point of a
question and not to waste their energy disentangling
the sense from the syntax.   Good questions should
also be no more and no less _specific_ that the examiner
intends them to be: some will specify in detail what
an essay should be about and how the question posed
should be handled, others are wide open.   A precise
and specific question should not be open to misinter-
pretation, an open question should be answerable at
several levels and in many ways.   Most questions fall
somewhere between, being intentionally open to a limited
number of interpretations;   all the essays will be more
or less about the same things.

"Essay questions ... should _encourage an extended res-
ponse_"; [1]   it should be impossible to break a question
down into a set of objective test items.   "(Finally)
it would appear uneconomical, in terms of time and
energy and in terms of the level of skill demanded in
handling the answers, to use essay tests for securing
information which can be obtained through short-answer
testing". [1]

Good essay titles and questions are _unambiguous_.   Many,
perhaps most, questions are neither very specific nor
completely open, but a question can be fairly general
without leaving the students uncertain as to whether
a broad or a narrow examination of a topic is expected.

As we have pointed out above, questions intended to
elicit particular responses or a particular kind of
response must always be accurately worded, but students
should be able to take any kind of question quite
literally.

Ambiguity sometimes arises from the unthinking use of
the traditional language of examining; students may
take a formal introductory phrase to be a precise instruction. Thus "Comment on ..." is conventionally an
invitation to analyse or to interpret a given passage,
but, used in subjects where a scholarly "commentary" is
an alien idiom, students may be at a loss as to what
they are intended to do. "Comment on the ground flora
of carboniferous limestones" - "Explain the origins
of...?", "Describe ...?", "Tell me what you find inter-
esting about ...?".

"Outline" and "significance" may also confuse. Take
"Outline the metabolic significance of Coenzyme A".
Are the students really intended to decide on the scope
and point of this question for themselves? At a first
reading this is a precise and specific question but is
"Outline" really a precise instruction, implying that a
fairly broad sweep of an answer is expected? Coenzyme
A is involved in many metabolic reactions; should a
broad sketch of the nature and range of these reactions
be followed by discussion of their general "significance"?
Or does "significance" lie in the particular nature of
the reactions so that a broad sketch of the role of
coenzymes in general, and of Coenzyme A in particular,
should be followed by detailed discussion of one or two
typical reactions, or as full and detailed a description

and discussion of as many reactions as time allows?

Many students will, perhaps justly, take this question
to be a general "Say what you know about Coenzyme A".
"Discuss" or "Comment on the metabolic significance of
Coenzyme A" would then have served the same purpose.
But why not put "What is the role of Coenzyme A in
intermediary metabolism?"?

Suppose now that the examiner had a more specific point
to the question in mind, and does not intend the question
to discriminate between students on the way in which they
interpret the question.   Such purposes should not be
hidden.   Why not "Coenzymes ..... What, _in these terms_,
is particularly significant about the metabolic role of
Coenzyme A?"

Sims[1] sees the broad "Discuss" type of question as a
stimulus - it is simply a means of generating an extended
response to the problematic situation.   But "Outline
(or discuss) the metabolic significance of Coenzyme A"
cannot function in this way; there is no problematic
situation.   Students taking their final examinations
will not be resolving the question of the metabolic significance of Coenzyme A; they are being asked to recall
what they have been taught.   However, at least it is
"metabolic significance" - "significance" often stands
alone.

Compare "Describe the main features of urban growth in
16th century England.   Discuss its significance." with
"Briefly describe the pentose phosphate pathway of
glucose metabolism.   Discuss its significance."   A

history student, practised in historical analysis,
should have a set of parameters within which to discuss
the significance of events ready to hand.   But a bio-
chemistry student may again be uncertain.   Should he
take his question to mean "Make a detailed comparison
of this alternative pathway with the main pathway of
glucose metabolism"?   Others, (perhaps more "clued
up")[10] may choose to take it to be about the general
significance of alternative pathways of metabolism and
use the pentose phosphate pathway, described very
briefly, as the principle illustration of their discussion.

We make these points to provoke argument.   When an
imprecise question is not the deliberate expression of
the examiner's intentions then problems arise with
marking.   Knowing how highly many examiners value
breadth of reading or of reference, skilled players of
the "examination game"[10] are often masters of the art
of bringing in unexpected points of information or of
widening a question in a way which its phrasing allows
but the examiner had not intended.   This cannot be
penalised, it may make the impression the games-player
hoped for.   But others who kept closer to the spirit
of the question may, by comparison, be penalised.   If
you write vague instructions in order to allow every
student to say what he wishes about a subject you should
determine beforehand whether or not marks are mainly
going to be awarded for how the question has been
tackled.   The more precise the formulation of the
question the less is the risk of receiving (particularly
from the fast writers) pages of stream-of-consciousness
response which are so difficult to assess.

The problem posed by an essay question should have a "reasonable separation from the original learning situation"[1] (our underlining). It is unusual to find students are presented with completely unfamiliar problematic situations but some degree of unfamiliarity is needed in most questions. "Reasonable separation from the original learning situation" means that students will not be able to give back what they have been taught in the form in which they received it, but that they will be able to progress by reference to what they have been taught.[3]

Every good question should be within the grasp of students of a <u>wide range of abilities</u>. Open questions in particular should be open to interpretation at different levels as well as in different ways. There is immense satisfaction for teacher and examiner in posing questions to challenge a new generation of student-scholars in their discipline, or indeed to so question individual students of ability. In coursework, especially when there is no formal assessment, individual students may be set, or may choose to take on, questions of variable depth and complexity. But in examinations it may be necessary to have a departmental ruling about the strictness of the equivalence to be maintained between questions.

We wish every student to give of his best and where there is a genuine choice of questions for each main topic in a syllabus it may be possible to set questions of different degrees of difficulty. Ideally students might perhaps be given a sufficiently wide choice for them to choose a question which both matches their ambitions and is compatible with the way they have come to view their subject.

But where there is little or no real choice (only one, or at most two, questions on each main topic) care must be taken, for example, not to use recondite terms or gnomic quotations; no question can be set with only the more able students in mind. Questions may discriminate between students of different ability on the grounds of how they interpret an open question but not on their familiarity with its wording or its source. The best of open questions are broad and provocative, searching and subtle. To be successful they should stimulate both intellect and imagination, but it must be possible for everyone to attempt them.

5. A CHECKLIST OF POINTS TO BE NOTED

Here is a list of points to consult when you review your essay titles or examination questions. Some are of greater importance when you are setting essays; others arise in the post-mortem. Look at your questions and titles through the eyes of your students. Remember that the post-mortem, though principally concerned with assessing the effectiveness of the student's learning, also gives you the opportunity to assess how well you have fulfilled your responsibilities. Good questions may occasionally produce outstanding answers; bad questions almost never do - apart from those daring answers which demonstrate the ineptness of the question.

Essays in Coursework

1. What is the point of this question? Is it clear from the wording?
2. What is the question supposed to cover? And to exclude? Are any limits you have set on the possible ways of answering the question made clear?
3. Is the area covered of sufficient importance to merit the work which the student will devote to this essay?
4. Is the question sufficiently demanding? Is it too demanding?
5. Are the sources needed for a good answer available? Have you made proper provision for access to books, journals, tutorial assistance?
6. Will students have to embark on the process of enquiry for themselves? You must decide how extensive and how detailed the tutorial and reference guidance you give them will be.
7. Will students have to use higher order intellectual skills in writing the essay? Will they (merely!) have to reproduce what they know, or have discovered? Or will they have to rearrange their knowledge or apply it to an unfamiliar problematic situation?
8. Is the title likely to result in 30 essays on very similar lines? Is that what you would wish to happen? If not, then how can you alter the wording to leave the mode of response more open?

When the essays have been taken in ask these questions again in the light of the evidence now before you. Further questions can then be asked.

9. Is there evidence of consistent misunderstanding of what the essay was intended to be about? How could the title have been framed to make this clearer, the question sharper?

10. Were the marks (if the essays were formally assessed) bunched? If so was this the fault of the marker as assessor or of the marker as question setter?

Essays in Examinations

An essay written in, say, 40 minutes under examination conditions is nevertheless an essay, and the list of points above can equally well be used to review examination questions. There are, however, additional questions you can usefully ask yourself about examination questions.

1. Is the question manageable in the time?
2. Does the question rely unduly on recall of data?
3. Do questions overlap? If so, is this to the extent that students can 'cash their chips' twice over?
4. Were any questions avoided by students?
5. Did the question elicit from some students their coursework essays? Is there a policy on this in your department?
6. Did each question discriminate in the sense of producing a spread of marks?

Finally, ask whether the students seem to have liked a title or question. Did you? A really good question is often intellectually and aesthetically pleasing to teachers, to examiners and to students. Students are more likely to give of their best, in our view, when

questions tickle their fancy in some way - they feel
pleased, expansive, and above all <u>responsive</u>. (Do you
know what kind of question might please a majority of
your students?)   Given such a question, especially in
his finals, a student may feel that this is what 'it'
was all about.   Fear of inadequacy fades, the stiff
locks of memory loosen, knowledge has meaning, understanding blossoms, the ink flows ...   We turn next
to "Marking".

PART III

MARKING

1. MARKING PROCEDURES

Marking essays in higher education is a complex and
intuitive business, often described as subject to a
hair-raising amount of caprice, but while it is difficult in general to mark essays reliably the evidence is
that marking by impression is not always significantly
less reliable than marking by other methods.[11] The
experienced examiner probably trusts almost entirely to
instinct; knowledge of the criteria and standards to
which he marks is in his bones; he knows what he wants
from each question and he is not going to be misled. A
new tutor or examiner needs to accumulate first-hand
experience of marking before he can make impressionistic
judgments with the same confidence; he may find it
easier to rely on systematic procedures to begin with.

Marking implies measurement and measurement implies comparisons. One yardstick you can use is a model answer
sketched in outline at the time of writing the question.
It will incorporate those salient points you think vital
to any complete answer to your question, and those
characteristics essential to any essay of this kind at
this level; this is more or less the best that could be
done with this question.

If your question was not detailed and explicit, however, the answers cannot be analysed in terms of expected characteristics and content.   When students give answers which are a distortion of what the examiner was looking for the problem is one of communication. [12]   The fault lies in the question and the question must now be treated as though it had not been intended to elicit a specific kind of essay.   But you cannot, in any case, often predetermine exactly what an essay is expected to consist of;   teachers and examiners in higher education seldom wish to ask narrow and specific questions.   Each essay must then be judged on its own merits and a model answer can serve only to confuse when perhaps only a few of the essays come anywhere near it.

The inexperienced marker may find it easiest to begin by making comparisons not with an imaginary ideal essay but between all the essays in a group before attempting to classify them in any way.   This can be done by several methods.   For example, essays can be placed in a rank order.   Or they can be sorted out by making distinctions between levels of quality until representative groups emerge. [3]   A third method would be to establish a mode by describing for yourself what the most straightforward, middle of the road way of answering a particular question would be. [1]   Look for essays which match this description;   other ways of answering, other kinds of answer, can then be grouped by judging them to be, for specific reasons, less satisfactory than the mode, or more satisfactory.

Before actual marks can be given to each essay some comparison must now be made against the internal standards of a discipline. Classification (or categorisation, since not all rating guides relate directly to degree classes) is the next step, and can be done by reference to a departmental guide to standards. (If none exists you can make one yourself in consultation with your colleagues.) For example:

"Grade   Description
A+/A   excellent critical and conceptual analysis/
               comprehensive survey of relevant issues/
               well argued/ well presented/ relevant
               reading effectively incorporated.
A-/B+/B   good critical and conceptual analysis/
               good survey of relevant issues/ satis-
               factory presentation/ relevant reading
               effectively incorporated.
B-/C+/C   rather more descriptive than critical &
               conceptual/ analysis lacks clarity in
               parts/ evidence of relevant reading but
               not always effectively used.
C-/D+   perfunctory/ largely descriptive/
               disorganised and lacking in detail.
D/D-   perfunctory/ almost entirely descriptive/
               narrow in conception/ poorly argued.
E   no evidence of understanding/ little
               evidence of a serious attempt.
O   not presented.

As a general and tentative guide a grade between A and B indicates a standard in the first or second class, B to C in the second or third class, C to D in the third to pass class, D. to D- in the pass/fail class and E or O an out-right fail."[13]

36

A guide of this kind needs to be drawn up with great
care for, ideally, each category would be sufficiently
well differentiated for there to be a clear relationship
between the mark given and the qualities of each essay.
It is easy to be brain-washed by some essays as you
read them; a guide is an essential defence against what
are called 'fudge factors'. Though general in tone the
example above is not a general guide; it is one used in
educational studies. In philosophy, mathematics and
history greater emphasis might be placed on argument,
conceptual precision is probably stressed in physics,
the understanding of reciprocal relationships in bio-
logical sciences. (Incidentally, whatever the principles may be which lie behind the class divisions in
any guide of this kind, do make sure that students know
and understand them.)

In many areas of study the only guide a new tutor is
given is a key to the relationship between a marking
scheme and degree classes; tutors are left to find
out or establish for themselves what the significant
differences are between, say, $\beta+$, β and $\beta-$ on the alpha-
beta scale. Such a guide can be set aside for the
moment; the inexperienced marker can best begin, in our
view, by placing essays on a rating scale with only a
few broad divisions. Begin with the degree class divisions, or with the classificatory 'descriptions' such as
those at the right hand side of the example above, and
match your ranked or grouped essays with these. It is
much easier to rate consistently on a 5-7 point scale
than it is on a 25-100 point scale. (There are usually
about 25 points on the alpha-beta scale, 100, of course,
on the % scale.) Indeed it is generally held to be

true that few people can ever consistently discriminate between more than 10 categories.[14] A further consideration is that the beginner is often marking coursework essays and a division or class mark may be all that is required.

But, having said this, the fewer the divisions then the more important the borderlines become, and it is going to be necessary always to take another look at all borderline cases - perhaps in consultation with a colleague. Another aspect of your classification which may warrant reconsideration is the way in which markers tend to lump most essays together as 'average' while avoiding the 'top' and 'unsatisfactory' categories.[3] There is, too, often an unspoken convention, nothing more than a feeling, within a discipline that a certain distribution within classes is proper to that discipline. (There is no deliberate adjustment of marks to fit norms.) Every member of a department will usually be guided by departmental standards and conventions. However, when the marks you give cluster too thickly about the middle of the range of possible marks then you may not be observing distinctions carefully enough. Examine the assumptions you personally have about low grades and about high ones.[3]

You can now go on to fine-grade within each division of your rating scale and to award marks on the familiar alpha-beta or % scales if this is required. Fine-grading can be based on impression or you may now prefer to consult a detailed checklist of criteria based on your intentions in setting each particular question - the detail of content, the abilities you set out to

examine, the characteristics you think important in
respect of different ways of tackling this question (or
this kind of question) and the general qualities you
look for in any essay.   This kind of list can, of course,
be derived from a model answer.

A checklist may be particularly useful for differentiating
between essays of closely comparable merit but if this
final exercise, and the consultation of a checklist, leads
you to reconsider your initial ranking or classification
of essays now is the time to ask a senior colleague for
his opinion.   No-one begins with an absolutely sure touch
and early in your career you will in any case be dependent
on second opinions.   (At least you should be!)   If
your department makes no formal provision for monitoring
your marks perhaps you can make an informal arrangement
for a colleague to double-mark your essays.

In the case of marks which 'count' it is sound practice
for all assessable work involving a significant element
of judgment to be double-marked, preferably blind, and
quite apart from marking by external examiners.   Even
if the second marker is not expert in the field concerned
the practice is worth maintaining;   the fact that there
is a second marker keeps the first marker alert.   From
the student's point of view, there is also then the
assurance that whenever significant discrepancies appear
between markers essays or examination scripts will be
given the careful re-reading they deserve and will be
drawn to the attention of the external examiner.

2. PRIOR CONSIDERATIONS

We would now like to take you back a step. Before
marking any essays it is worth giving some thought to
questions about the setting of standards, which face
every teacher and examiner. What in general is to be
rewarded, what is to be penalised and what is to be
condoned in students' essays? The style of typical
undergraduate essays make it impossible for a scholar
unequivocally to judge them using his usual criteria.

The editor of The Times has described the nature of
undergraduate essays.[(15)]   Their "broad arguments and
sweeping statements" might be unacceptable to the
scholar, are they to the teacher and examiner?   If you
do mark them down, do you do so evenly?   There could
well be a tendency for some individual markers to penalise
the better undergraduate essays proportionately more than
the average essays.   Are the first essays you mark in a
group treated more harshly than those you come to later?

We are also told that students' essays lack "a sense of
proportion so that trivial details, themselves introduced
as evidence of research effort, are accorded equal weight
with matters of great importance" and they use "supposedly
telling quotations from a limited number of sources of
different value".   To what extent are you going to reward,
to condone or to penalise this kind of material in a
student's essay?

Most markers are concerned with the quality of the argument and of the analysis in an essay, but undergraduates,
according to the editor of The Times, often combine

"superficial plausibility with the absence of any real grasp of the subject matter". Suppose one or two of your students show real grasp, do you mark <u>them</u> against 'real'criteria and the superficially plausible against another set representing what is, say, good, fair, adequate and poor argument for an undergraduate?

We can only ask questions; we cannot write a rulebook. However let us look more closely at some of these problems. First that of relevance - this is always tricky. Every essay title or examination question has a point to it and that point should be one which the average student in your class can understand. Now whether or not each student grasps the point, all essays will furnish some evidence of what has been learned and are, therefore, useful to the teacher. But every answer which does not actually answer the question is a problem for the examiner.

It is important to attempt to analyse why the student missed the point. Was the wording of the question imprecise? Was the student being 'too clever by half' and using adjacent material already used elsewhere or shifting the question to one he would have preferred to answer? Is this a case of the student who answers every question by writing down all he can remember about the topic? Obviously if this happens with a course essay it is important to have an individual tutorial, no matter how brief, in order to identify the cause and apply a remedy. The response is individual and the corrective should be individualised.

Not all students who seem to have missed the point have done so through error or lack of ability. Some will have deliberately missed it and should be firmly directed away from the slippery path that leads towards roguery.

The student's academic standing has also to be taken into account and some tutors in non-assessable coursework give what are called 'therapeutic' (a euphemism for over-generous) marks to students whom they feel should be encouraged. The use of such marks for work which is part of the formal assessment is, of course, quite wrong, but something of this spirit inevitably persists. It is common experience that in any course involving subjective assessment the mean of the coursework gradings will be higher than that for the examination gradings. Such patterns may give some students a false idea of their standing and of their academic prospects. It cannot be too often repeated that there are dangers in allowing confusion between the roles of teacher and of examiner.

Departments sometimes establish corporate principles of good practice for dealing with irrelevant essays within classes. It is easy, for example, to decide how to mark a well-written but off-the-point essay; someone who can write well is also able enough to write cogently (if he has done the work) and should be penalised if he does not.

A department may decide to declare which qualities in an essay merit placing it within a particular class; there should similarly be agreement about what factors prevent an essay from being admitted to a class. Thus, "No tutor would give a first class mark, and very few would give a IIi mark, to an essay which contained substantial irrelevance, unless there had been an excusable misunder-standing of the question".[16]

42

The departmental note to all staff and students which
we have just quoted goes on to discuss the balance between desirable and undesirable qualities in an essay.
In historical essays, it says, it is usual to penalise
narrative. (In environmental sciences, on the other
hand, a clear and connected exposition of complex factual
material may be just what the examiners want.) The
ability to substantiate an argument is important, but
this means including in an essay only carefully selected
telling points. Narrative is "destructive of effective
argument. Even odd patches of narrative must seriously
affect continuity and coherence." And "Where narrative
is interspersed with incidental comment a low IIii might
just be earned - though the comment would have to be
bright enough to justify it!" On the other hand "Few
markers would go above β+ (a middle IIi) for the essay
which may be bright and fluent but which lacks the
trenchancy which only evidence and example can give."
Clearly there are nice distinctions to be made and it is
right that students should be alerted to the criteria
being used.

Some critics of traditional examining practices feel
that by and large we are prepared to condone too much that
is unsatisfactory, not to penalise work in which (to
continue the discussion above) "paraphrase predominates
over real analysis".[2]   Above all there may be too
much readiness to admit essay work of little real merit
to the honours lists. We are very careful in distin-
guishing work of real quality but is as much attention
paid to the III/Pass boundary as is paid to the I/IIi?[17]

One way both of getting round and of capitalising upon

reluctance to downgrade students' work is to follow the example of the German department at Warwick University[2] where the only work which is formally assessed is re-worked essays. If you wish only to assess each student's best work here is a way of doing so. Obviously, in such cases the criteria are those appropriate to such re-worked essays.

Finally there is a distinction to be made in all these considerations between examination and coursework essays. The same basic principles of assessment apply to both, allowance being made for the different circumstances surrounding each situation. It is not usually the case that examiners look for any radically different qualities, but more is expected of coursework essays in certain respects and less is condoned. For example, the presentation of an argument in a coursework essay would be expected to be supported by a wider range of more extensive quotations or references accurately referenced, whereas in an essay written under examination conditions outlines would be accepted in place of proofs and allusions rather than quotations.

3. RELIABILITY

No examiner is ready to concede that his marks are only a rough and ready measurement; they are intended to be an accurate expression of what he judges the merit of each essay to be. But if essays cannot be marked consistently then they are less effective measures of whatever they are intended to measure, and there is ample evidence that essay tests are of poor reliability.[18] (The reliability of a test is the consistency with which

44

it measures.)

In order to improve reliability more precise questions can be asked, requiring shorter answers which are open to analytic marking, but these are not the kind of questions an examiner in higher education would ask when he is using essays to their best advantage. It _is_ possible either to fragment some questions, examples would be questions 1,2 and 7 in the Appendix, or to pre-determine the proportionate distribution of marks between the parts of such a question so that you would virtually be marking a set of shorter questions.

However can we "uncritically transfer to essay testing the 'principles' determining reliability which have been evolved in objective testing"?[1]   Sims suggests that reliability may be improved by placing greater emphasis on the representativeness of the essays assessed.   When students have reworked essays with tutorial guidance before submitting them[2] it seems likely that the work assessed will be more represen-tative of the best of each student's work.

While there is unease about the difficulty of marking essays consistently there is no general disquiet about the accuracy of degree results based, often in large part, on essay marks.   Marks for individual essays represent only one judgment of the calibre of a student's work and the degree class he is awarded is a consensus arrived at through the accommodation of the judgments of his different examiners.   Marks are moderated; it may be that variations in marking are brought within acceptable limits during this process.   This would not mean, of course, that marking could become a casual affair. Every effort should always be made by the individual examiner to mark as accurately and as consistently as possible and every effort should be made to harmonise the bases of judgment between markers. Marking and the review and combination of marks should be orderly and systematic.

Which sources of variation in marks can an examiner guard against? One of the difficulties facing you will be that of establishing any fixed criteria against which to assess essays, particularly at final degree level. Where such criteria can be agreed they should be thoroughly discussed; it is one thing to have, for example, stylistic criteria, quite another matter to have them interpreted in the same way.

Then there is the problem of differences of opinion about, say, the relative importance of the different elements in any one essay and, indeed, about the relative merits of different essays. Judgment of essays remains essentially subjective and all essays are of relative merit, it being impossible to define any single answer as complete and correct.[3] The individual examiner must therefore be at great pains to make his judgment both careful and honest.

Lastly there is the need always to be conscious of the danger of reading qualities into an essay, either those based on personal knowledge of its author or those resulting from your interpretation of what the student has written. Try never 'to go beyond the data.'

4. PREPARING ESSAYS FOR RETURNING THEM TO STUDENTS

This section is entirely about coursework essays.
Although coursework essays are now often assessed formally
as part of many degree schemes, as a tutor turns to thinking about returning each essay to his students he may yet
be far from the pressures of, for example, academic league
tables. It is to be hoped that he will remain so; this
is the point at which his teaching role takes precedence.
It is to be hoped, also, that he will not too quickly
adopt 'professional' habits.

This part is about marking, this section is about your
comments upon individual student's essays. You will not,
therefore, be concerned here with the best ways of handling essays, nor with the best essays, but with how to
help and to encourage each student to achieve the best
he is capable of - a formidable responsibility. But
though it can be burdensome, the detailed marking of
essays can be an enjoyable and rewarding task. We
spoke in the introduction to this booklet of the need
for pragmatic compromises between what you would, ideally,
wish to do with essays, and what you can manage to do.
It may be helpful to think about different levels,
different degrees of thoroughness and care with which
essays can be marked. It then becomes possible to
recognise the level you are at and to see what more you
could do in the way of attempting to move just one level
higher for an expenditure of time and energy you <u>can</u>
reasonably afford.

We do not wish to lay down principles and, of course,
we cannot construct a step by step 'Guide to Better

Marking'. As you get to know your students, so you will always be the best judge of what help they need and what they expect. And you will always be the best judge of where each one can be expected to make improvements, which faults or weaknesses may be irremediable and therefor not to be overstressed in comments, which areas or aspects of a subject are being neglected, when to be severe with your criticism, when to praise. On the other hand we do not wish to begin by setting out the least you could do - so we offer a sketch of the ideal.

We first list the three separate acts we see as the constituents of the expression of judgment on an essay. We then describe the fullest possible comments which could be made on just two of the features of an essay, supposing for the moment that tutors have inexhaustible reserves of patience, willingness and time. We hope you will look critically at this sketch and think about how you would choose to mark and to comment on essays in ideal circumstances. Thereafter we acknowledge that circumstances are unlikely to be ideal and ask questions about what you actually could do.

There are then, in our view, three separate parts to the expression of judgment:
* the mark;
* a summing up of the essay's strengths, weaknesses and all-round merit;
* more detailed comments about what is or is not well done, with suggestions for further learning.

The mark is an expression of the essay's worth as compared with the work of the author's peers and in

relation to general academic standards within a discipline. The summing up explains the grounds for giving
the mark. With experience marking and summing up
comments can be made fairly quickly and fairly easily;
marking is based on general impression so the description of the main features of each essay is being formed
as it is being read through for the first time. The
summing up will often be made in terms of comparisons.
"This essay is reasonably well organised"; standards
are implied.

Detailed comments then possibly consist of drawing the
student's attention to those points which collectively
shaped the marker's judgment. In the body of the
essay there may be actual underlinings, 'good points',
the arrowing of weaknesses, and corrections of small
errors. This kind of marking can become very practised.
Individual essays, with time, begin to fall into categories; the strengths and weaknesses of this type or of
that type are familiar, the comments are ready.

Now turn the whole thing upside down. There is a name,
not a number, attached to a coursework essay. The
essay may be one of a type but the essayist has written
only this. (It may be all that he or she will ever
have the chance of writing about this topic with the
certain expectation of being answered.) What can you
say to this student about this essay which will be of
benefit to him?

An ideal treatment
If thinking about the essay from the student's point of
view means changing your frame of reference completely

you may need to read the essay a second time. Mark and
summing up still go together - at the head or the end of
the essay; a placing judgement is still necessary.
But you may now wish to add a further remark to the
summing up which is a personal encouragement or exhor-
tation of some kind, relating this essay to this student's
work elsewhere or to his previous achievements. "You
are really beginning to get to grips with the question
of ..., now ...". If there is a lot to say about the
essay's and the essayist's faults and virtues then you
probably make a second set of general remarks beneath
and separate from the judgment. These teaching notes
will be part discussion, part analysis, and will be
based on and reinforced by detailed comments in the text
of the essay.

The teacher's main effort goes into looking for ways of
ensuring the student learns all that he can from this
essay and of improving his future work. This means
stopping to think about the essay rather than simply
making mental or marginal notes of its plus and minus
features. How ambitious is the essay? If the essayist has fallen short of what he set out to achieve, by
how much has he done so and why? If he has tackled
complex ideas but failed to disentangle them, perhaps
you can give him some guidance on how to marshal his
thoughts more effectively. If individual ideas are mis-
handled perhaps this is a fault of expression. Let us
look at the two examples of the style and the construction
of an essay.

First, style. It is often said that there is an eternal
triangle of teacher, taught and subject; at each point

of it there are reciprocal relationships with both of
the other two. Reading an essay, the tutor is listen-
ing to the student. How derivative is his language?
Point out where he uses direct and vivid expressions
which show you that he has understood the meaning of
what he is discussing. And explain what you are re-
marking upon - it isn't just the neat phrase that has
attracted attention, as he might think if you put "I
like the way you have expressed this". Instead say
"You've really got the point when you put it in your
own words like this".

But if there are signs of a personal style developing
do put "I like the way you express this"! Is the
style unnecessarily involved, the language obscure?
Does he require 'help' rather than 'facilitating
assistance'? Has he incorporated chunks of borrowed
language into his essay? Perhaps he has failed to distinguish the idea itself from the context of details and
phrases in which he found it. [19] Can you clearly see
the precise point that is relevant? Put it down un-
adorned and as simply as possible above his weighty
hidden quotation. Is he embroidering too much? (Perhaps
earlier attempts to write in a more colourful style were
praised.) Say "It's a nice touch but don't embroider
things too much" or "This is overdoing things. If you are
going to embroider to this extent you might try using a
few subtler shades and finer threads."

Next, construction. Search incoherence for the relation the student is trying to perceive, perhaps, between
one part of the essay and another. Then bring out your
coloured pencils. Suppose he is trying to balance two

ways of looking at something, perhaps opposing masses of
evidence, but has failed to show quite what is a counter-
weight to what.   Ring the points on one side of the
balance in red, on the other side in black and establish
the tension between opposing points by drawing a line
between them.

Is there a better way of ordering the steps in his argument?   Number them in the margin.   Mark the central
ideas with an asterisk or ring the growth points with a
coloured pencil (green?).   Link up the flow of the
central ideas by arrowed lines (blue?).   Bracket parts
that could be reduced and put a pair of upward and down-
ward pointing arrows in the margin where a point could
be expanded.

We are not suggesting that you rewrite the essay but
early in a course students may benefit a great deal from
having an occasional essay analysed with this care and
in this kind of detail.   "Essay weaknesses come in many
types; and one might hazard the generalisation that the
more serious they are, the earlier they occur in the
intellectual process of essay-writing.   Thus failure to
cite appropriate evidence is almost a matter of cosmetics -
a last-minute thing - but irrelevance or illogical argu-
mentation set in somewhere much earlier down the line;
and the most damaging error of all is failure to disentangle the meaning of the question itself".[20]

At a more realistic level?
It can be rather difficult repeatedly to summon up the
interest and responsiveness our ideal treatment requires
of a tutor.   (We have not forgotten that he needs time

for other things and that his many other activities are also a drain on his energy.) An excellent essay is the easiest to respond to; you pick up its points with relish, capping its neat instances and witty asides with examples of your own.   You think about its perspectives and add a note on some book or other which will extend the thinking that lies behind this essay.   The really poor essay calls for careful tutorial marking, remedial reading and notes about the basic factors to be observed in writing any essay of this kind.   But the general run of essays are only moderately good and these are the ones which sometimes receive scant attention.

Suppose, now, that you are not prepared to attempt the kind of close and sympathetic reading of each essay which we have just been discussing.   You can still expand your summing up to include one or two personally helpful remarks.   What are they to be based on?

It would be simple to pick out and to concentrate on each essay's obviously best and worst features.   Look for where improvement could be made and show how it could be done.   Look for missed opportunities and for growth points - show how these could be developed; never make adverse criticisms without suggesting remedies. What is more deadening that the isolated remark "Try to get a better balance."? How? Between what? It is just as destructive to say "You've almost exactly hit the mark." Precisely what _is_ the mark?   If the essayist were shown it he might make a better shot if he is ever asked to aim at a mark like this again.   "Reasonably sound argument."   The student looks at his essay again and it is much as it was before.   He knows now that it is a reasonably sound argument but he still knows of no other. What does he learn from this? Look, too, for signs of ability to commend.

Where an essay has no notable features and provokes little response you may like to try checking it against the kind of list of stylistic criteria, points of importance or of content which is sometimes used as a marking aid. An essay is more than the sum of its parts but if it has no engaging faults or virtues you can at least check the parts. A moderately detailed resume of the essay's commonplace merits and demerits can quickly be drawn up and you can then pick out one or two to deal with more fully - looking at them now with the sympathy of a tutor.

Take "evidence of relevant reading, not always effectively used", for example. This could become, "You have included the main points but in substantiating them you do not make their relative importance clear, but see below". Marginal notes will then show why some of the evidence cited is shaky or where support for a point is too thin. Do this with care and the student can learn a great deal from the exercise. The tutor can set his own limits on how detailed the checking is to be and on how exhaustive the treatment of the chosen features.

Beard[21] suggests that a general list of numbered evaluatory criteria could be drawn up and circulated to students; tutors interested in this idea might try drawing up a series of numbered comments appropriate to their subject. If every student has a copy then the tutor's written remarks may simply consist of a list of numbers.

Procedures of this kind may seem to trivialise the
tutor's role and may seem too mechanical for use in
higher education, but feedback is enormously important
to students; is a mark and/or a general comment really
enough? Apparently there is positive improvement in
students' essays as a result simply of listing points
(this could be done quite quickly and at random) under
the two headings "Good" and "Unsatisfactory".[21]

An acceptable minimum
At the very least, then, you will add to your judgment
one or two remarks on each essay which show you have
looked at it from within the student's frame of reference. And where necessary you have explained all your
remarks by reference to details in the text of the
essay as fully as you have time to do. There will be
little point, of course, in making too much of the ways
in which this particular essay could have been improved,
or understanding of this particular theme could be
enhanced, either when study of it is complete or when
you have no intention of returning the essays until the
course unit is running to its close.

This is what we feel to be an acceptable minimum, but the
need for written, tutorial comment on students' essays
is by no means accepted by everyone. Some may feel that
detailed comment is unnecessary; part of the learning
exercise is to examine an essay in the light of a tutor's
general remarks. Others may feel detailed comment to be
unnecessary because the teacher's response is made in
tutorial and seminar meetings. Others again feel that

it is a waste of time - students do not want it. "Once
it's done it's a sort of death - you don't want to see
it again; you want to disassociate yourself from the
thing altogether; so his constructive criticism, I'm
afraid it falls on deaf ears rather".[10]   Learning
can be a painful business but teachers learn to be
patient and pertinacious.   Can you persuade him to pick
it up again?   Should you?   We leave you with the
questions.

An unforgivably low level of response
It is quite unforgivable to fail to mark and return
essays quickly when they have been written during a
course of study as a learning exercise, regardless of
whether or not the marks contribute to formal assessment.
"It's usually a month since you've written it and you
can't even remember what the question was, never mind
what you've written, and the tutor says, 'Yes, well I
think you were wrong at this point or that point' and
you don't really care, you want to get the mark."[10]

If you cannot easily find time to mark essays quickly
and thoroughly most students would probably be glad if
you were to make your position clear from the beginning -
essays will not be returned quickly, though they will get
them back in time for revision, and you will give only
a brief general summary of worth.   You enjoy reading
their essays and what you get from them will be reflected
in other teaching situations, but once they have handed
them in that is really that.   Surely this would be
better than stringing them along in weekly expectation of
getting their essays back?

Follow up

How do you return essays? It is not often possible
nowadays to have regular one to one tutorials, but many
tutors regard this as so important, especially when
returning the first essay on a new course, that they will
contrive to hold such tutorials even if they only last
for 20 minutes. During a tutorial the tutor has the
opportunity to explore an essay topic thoroughly with a
student, to build on what has been learned, to respond
positively to any interest expressed in this or that
aspect of a subject. It is easy to reach for a book or
to spend a couple of minutes on a pointed anecdote that
would be tedious to write out. And in an atmosphere
that suits him a student may risk jokes, ask questions,
question comments. Writing an essay may be so formal
and serious a business to some that they would never
include in it anything unorthodox or any of their own
views.

However, if they were practically possible, regular
personal tutorials would not always be welcomed; tutors
and students do not always find each other congenial.
Here are some alternatives:
* essays can be left in a general office for
  students to pick up;
* students may be required to come and collect
  their essays from a table in their tutor's
  room - they then have the opportunity to
  talk about the essay if they wish;
* small group tutorials for the discussion of
  essays can be formally included in timetables
  (3-4 friends can then arrange to come together);
* there can be voluntary tutorials; (the tutor

57

makes a warm, general and open invitation to
students either to make an appointment with
him, individually or in groups, or to come
without prior arrangement at specified hours
during the week);

* individual students can be given a strong
  nudge; "I think it would be in your best
  interest to come and discuss this with me.
  I might be able to help you to make more
  sense out of Indifference Curves and this
  could certainly be to your advantage when
  we go on from there next term";

* or a carrot; you really feel that it is
  absolutely necessary to see this student,
  "β+/α-?   Come and convince me of the α
  quality."

PART IV

ESSAY WRITING

In coursework the teaching and learning and the assessment functions of essays overlap, indeed they conflict
at many points. Where they do so this is to the detri-
ment of teaching and learning. It has been persuasively
argued that the increased use of coursework assessment
coupled with the spread of teaching through group
seminars has resulted in a tendency to under-rate the
place of the essay in shaping the development of the
individual student as a scholar.[20] Certainly the
fact that an increasing proportion of a student's written
work is submitted as part of the formal assessment has
the effect of stressing the tutor's role as assessor.
No teacher deliberately subordinates learning to assessment but the new lecturer should perhaps be warned of
the need to guard against drifting into a situation
where circumstances compel him to be more examiner than
teacher. We have made a point of emphasising what can
be done to correct this drift. Now we would like to
end with a brief consideration of ways of teaching, or
of helping students to improve, essay writing _per_ _se_.

It is often assumed that students know how to write
essays, and the difference between good and unsatisfactory essays, before they enter higher education. This
is a questionable assumption. First year students and
those who move between disciplines or across disciplinary

boundaries will not always be experienced essay writers. Besides it is not evident that everyone who has prac- tised has yet perceived or been shown the difference between what, in general terms, is good essay writing, and what is not.   Students are judged on their essays. What can be done to ensure that no-one is handicapped from the start by their ignorance of good essay-writing techniques?

Students will, of course, learn from your comments on their essays.   The general summing up of the merit of an essay enables its author to see it through other eyes. More detailed comments, intended to be more directly helpful, may indeed be so.   (Commenting on essays has been fully dealt with in the preceding section.)   But to be of actual benefit written tutorial comment must be capable of translation into <u>action by the essayist himself</u>. For example, it is more helpful to say "When answering a question of this kind it is better to make a point by point comparative analysis, rather than to deal with each party separately making your comparison only in general terms in your final paragraphs. Look back at your notes on my lecture about reform movements and compare my treatment of that theme with the way you have presented this", than it is to say "The comparison could be more detailed".

What more can be done?   <u>A tutorial</u> early in the session could be devoted to outlining techniques of good essay writing, showing the pupil how to organise material and the kind of questions he must ask himself.   Either individual or group tutorials could be used - even an illustrated lecture showing in parallel "What we like in essays" and "What we do not like". (There might be a market for a really good, light, snappy and fully illustrated 'Students' Guide to Approved Essay Techniques'.) You may dislike the emphasis on "What we like" but this is a carrot many students respond to.

The more illustrative examples you can produce the better and, whether or not you have time for a teaching session, these can always be circulated or made available for interested students to consult. The best models might well be those culled from undergraduate essays ("What they can do I can do") but chapters from books can be cited, passages from journals can be reproduced, and used as "a means of identifying and exemplifying particular qualities". [20] It might even be possible to keep whole essays on file (with all signs of authorship removed but with the marks they were given and tutor's comments left on them). The selected essays would be typical both of good work and of common types of less satisfactory essay writing. Both models of this kind and the general qualities which are deemed to be important in the writing of essays should be related to academic standards.

It is quite common to circulate a key relating qualities of essays to departmental marking schemes. (An example is on page 36). In some departments much fuller notes for the guidance of both staff and students are handed out. (We have quoted from one such handout on page 42.)

Primed by all this information students may sometimes welcome the opportunity to practise specific skills, either for themselves or under supervision, before

or in between writing full essays. You could set them
short exercises, perhaps a library exercise on the selection of evidence, an exercise in weighing evidence you
have collected, a comparison and evaluation of sources,
or the writing of a number of essay outlines to practise
organising material in response to specific questions.
Or, given the kind of checklist of stylistic criteria
you might use in marking essays, they could be set to
assessing anonymous essays from earlier years or material
from published texts. Any of these could be self-
assessed exercises if model answers were provided.

However all this would entail a lot of work on the part
of the tutor who might prefer to incorporate any exercise of this kind which he thought worthwhile into the
work he does with students in preparation for the
assignments he actually sets them. Thus while he might
ask them to draft an outline of an essay, or to present
a list of sources, these would be looked at, or discussed
with individual students, as a means of monitoring their
preparation for essays. Some tutors still find time to
hold individual or small group tutorials while essays
are in the process of being written, seeing this as an
important means of helping students to produce the best
they are capable of for assessment. We have, of course,
already cited the Warwick University German Department's
innovatory scheme wherein essays are presented, sometimes
as seminar papers, fully discussed and reworked with
tutorial guidance before being formally submitted for
assessment. [2]

Some tutors like to encourage students to read each
others' essays and this can be done informally both

before and after they are marked.   A set of essays on
related themes might be circulated, before they are
marked, to a seminar group prior to a meeting.   The
students can discuss flaws and points of interest in
each other's work; their understanding of each other's
viewpoints will be enhanced.   They may begin to see a
topic in the round.   They may also learn something
about self-assessment in relation to criteria other than
grades and sharpen their insights into their own academic
development and postures.   This has been described as an
effective learning strategy for language translations.[22]
An alternative strategy would be to use students' con-
tributed notes, on specific points or aspects of a topic,
in a seminar or group meeting as the material for an
"essay-writing simulation exercise".

However, not every tutor was a typical student and if you
recognise that, lacking instinctive understanding of
students' learning problems, you may not be the person
best qualified to teach them about the process of learning,
you may wish to encourage your students to make use of the
support services your institution may provide.   In
addition to counselling services for individual students
you may find either that there are study skills courses
on offer or that study skills seminars can be set up by
an educational services unit on request.   These are
likely to cover topics like reading effectively, taking
notes and constructing sound arguments as well as essay
writing techniques.

And last of all, tell every one of your students about
the "keys to success".   "What a difference it makes to
the speed and ease of marking if the essays are typed

rather than hand-written. Now that continuous assessment is increasingly displacing the classic three-hour finals paper as a method of examining undergraduates, is it too much to expect that students entering the university should as a matter of course acquire and learn to use a typewriter (which can, after all, be bought for about the same sum as a cheap record-player)?

There is no simpler way, I believe, of increasing the efficiency and productivity of university teachers in the humanities at a time when understaffing is a serious problem in many departments. My own department, I am pleased and proud to say, has, through the initiative of a few colleagues, taken a step in the right direction by organizing self-financing group-tuition in typing by a professional instructor. But a broad-based campaign seems required. Dons for Typed Essays, perhaps, with lapel buttons that declare I LIKE TYPE."[23]

APPENDIX - EXAMPLES OF EXAMINATION QUESTIONS AND ESSAY TITLES

(This list begins with precise and specific questions and is
arranged roughly in the order of increasing openness of questions.)

1. Describe the Monte Carlo technique used to shed light on the
   small sample properties of various estimation methods. Review
   the main results of the Monte Carlo studies with which you are
   familiar. In the light of these results discuss the choice
   of estimation methods in Econometrics.

2. Undertake a stylistic analysis of ONE of the following passages,
   selecting, arranging and commenting on features of syntax, lexis,
   semantics and (where relevant) phonology, in order to relate the
   artistic effects of the passage to the writer's choice of
   language. (Comments and observations may be made in note form
   if lack of time forbids a more formal presentation.)

3. Plants respond to light using pigments and mechanisms that are
   apparently unrelated to photosynthesis. Discuss how these
   light reactions regulate growth and development so increasing
   the chance of survival in different environments.

4. Analyse the difference between Locke's and Froebel's use of
   play in the education of young children.

5. Assess Richard as a strategist and statesman in the light of
   the expedition to Ireland in 1394.

6. Analyse and compare the attitude towards death, whether of the
   author, the protagonists and/or particular classes of society,
   in any three or more of the following passages at least one of
   which must be poetry.

7. Write explanatory notes on FOUR of the following terms.

   (a) Anavamala   (e) Maṇḍala

   (b) Avidyā   (f) Prakṛti

   (c) Ekagratā   (g) Tapas

   (d) Japa   (h) Yuga

8. "The autobiographical method in Jane Eyre works so well that the
   many shifts of narrative viewpoints, which make it succeed, go
   unnoticed."
   Consider the purpose and effectiveness of "shifts of narrative
   viewpoint" in either Jane Eyre or Wuthering Heights or
   Middlemarch or Bleak House or Vanity Fair.

9. "Although a good case can be made for free trade on the grounds of economic efficiency, there is no case on the grounds of equity". Discuss.

10. Account for the dichotomy between the aims and practice of the German Working Class Movement between 1871 and 1914.

11. What is the purpose of the Codes of Botanical and Zoological Nomenclature? Discuss whether these objectives can ever be achieved.

12. Should industrial training be subsidised?

13. We often speak of 'Tolstoyan' qualities when referring to particular kinds of novelistic achievement. How would you define, exemplify and evaluate such qualities from your own knowledge of Tolstoy's work?

14. Why no self in Buddhism?

15. What problems face the linguist in the description of a Creole language continuum?

16. "Even after Locke's book was written the subject remained almost untouched and I fear that my book will leave it pretty much as it found it." (Rousseau: the preface to Emile.) Did Rousseau leave education as he found it?

17. "The Phillips curve, if it exists at all, is a vertical straight line". Discuss.

18. Does Donald Evans save his position by onlooks?

19. Is variation ever selectively neutral?

20. The South is a minority. Does the literature of the South present us with a separate distinctive world?

21. "Though conceptually suspect and empirically unsupported elite theories remain remarkably persuasive." Discuss.

22. Are the Jeremiads plausible sources for the social historian?

23. Is literalism a symptom of a dose of Flew?

24. What flavour can a religion impart, plausibly, to goodness?

25. "A salutory level of explanation is reached when the intelligent man calls 'Stop'." Discuss.

26. Is it sensible to ask, or possible to answer, why there is anything at all?

27. Write an essay on "Integration and isolation in nature."

****

Questions 4 and 16 are taken from:

Educational Studies Course 302 - Essays, Michaelmas Term 1975 (unpublished)
University of Lancaster, Department of Educational Research.

All the remaining questions are taken from:

Part II (Final Year) Examinations for the Degree of Bachelor of Arts (or of Science).   University of Lancaster (1970-1976).

REFERENCES

1. SIMS, V.M. (1948) "The essay examination as a projective technique"
   Educational and Psychological Measurement 8: pp. 15-31.
2. THOMAS, R.H. (1976) "The necessity of examinations - and their reform"
   Studies in Higher Education 1 (1): pp. 23-29.
3. STALNAKER, J.M. (1951) in LINDQUIST, E.F. (Ed.) *Educational Measurement*
   Washington, D.C. American Council of Education.
4. BROCKBANK, P. (1968) "Examining exams"
   The Times Literary Supplement No. 3465: pp. 781-782.
5. THOMAS, L. & AUGSTEIN, S. (1970) *An Experimental Approach to Learning from Written Material*
   Uxbridge. Centre for the Study of Human Learning, Brunel University.
6. KNOX, J.D. (1975) *The Modified Essay Question: Booklet No.5*
   Dundee. Association for the Study of Medical Education.
7. SELLEN, R.W. (1976) "The 'Open Question' and student design of part of the course"
   Improving College and University Teaching XXIV (3): p. 155.
8. Educational Studies Course 302: Essays - Michaelmas Term 1975 (unpublished).
   University of Lancaster. Department of Educational Research.
9. BLACK, B.J. (1968) "University examinations"
   Physics Education 3 (2): pp. 93-99.
10. MILLER, C.M.L. & PARLETT, M. (1974) *Up to the Mark: a study of the Examination Game*
    London. S.R.H.E.
11. WISEMAN, W. (1949) "The marking of English composition in grammar school selection"
    British Journal of Education Psychology 19: pp. 200-209.
12. JACKSON, D. & JACQUES, D. (Eds.) (1976) *Improving Teaching in Higher Education*
    London. U.T.M.U.
13. Guide to Part I Tutors (unpublished)
    University of Lancaster. Department of Educational Research.
14. This rule of thumb is given in all the standard texts. See, for example:
    LINDQUIST, E.F. (Ed.) (1951) *Educational Measurement*
    Washington D.C. American Council for Education.
15. *The Times,* 8 September 1976.
16. HOLMES, G. (unpublished) "Essays, Exams and All That": a handout circulated to both staff and students.
    University of Lancaster. History Department.
17. JONES, P.M. (1965) "The fallacies of the examination system"
    Universities Quarterly 19: pp. 240-258.